THE
ILLUSTRATIONS

Books by Norman Dubie

THE BRAZILLER SERIES OF POETRY
Richard Howard, General Editor

THE ILLUSTRATIONS

Poems by

NORMAN DUBIE

with a note by Richard Howard

GEORGE BRAZILLER

New York

Some of these poems have previously appeared in the following publications, to whose editors grateful acknowledgment is made: *The American Poetry Review, Arion's Dolphin, The North American Review, Grilled Flowers, The Black Warrior Review, Antaeus, The Iowa Review, The Presumpscot, The Seneca Review, The Antioch Review, Twelve Poems, Field,* and *Uzzano.*

Some of these poems appeared first in a limited edition volume, *Popham of the New Song,* The Graywolf Press, 1975.

IBIS and THE NEGRESS: HER MONOLOGUE OF DARK CRÊPE WITH EDGES OF LIGHT originally appeared in *Poetry.*

SUN AND MOON FLOWERS: PAUL KLEE, 1879–1940 AND FEBRUARY: THE BOY BREUGHEL both appeared first in *The New Yorker.*

Dubie, Norman, 1945–
    The illustrations.
    (The Braziller series of poetry)
    I. Title.
PS3554.U25514   811'.5'4   76–16637
ISBN 0-8076-0857-2
ISBN 0-8076-0858-0 pbk.

First Printing
Printed in the United States of America
Designed by Kathleen Carey

Contents

NORMAN DUBIE

"Some inevitable sadness that will visit each of us"

What are they illustrations *of*, these irregular, even rugged but
ever rutilant poems in Norman Dubie's third book? The word
itself will tell us, for we regard being, even our own being, as
illustrious when it is purified and illuminated by light—when it
is lustrated. But is it our being which is in question, and in an-
swer, here? Look down the table of contents: from Lascaux to
D. H. Lawrence, from a painting by Van de Velde to a novel by
Gide, these poems of Dubie's are "brief lives" of other people,
hell itself (as Hegel said), invited into the poet's own speech,
invented by the poet's own words in one of the great Flirtation
Routines of our moment. Or is it always the poet's life, as the
insistent dedications to family and friends suggest . . . a world of
derived identities?

If I ask so many questions, it is because so many answers are
afforded by the poems, because so much light is cast, is shed by
the poems themselves that we are choked, blinded: we know too
much. For example, we know what it is like to be Horace on the
Sabine farm ("the Goths have been defeated, and Maecenas was
his friend"):

> Here in the hills
> Caesar is a spectacle of dead trout
> Washed with smashed mint and lemons.
> What have I kept back?
> Only this: there is no way to leave him.

And we know what it is like to be Aleksandr Blok ("at night St.
Petersburg is empty"):

> Once when you were very young you watched peasants
> Shoot a horse in a pasture: it fell over
> Like a table. And what I've kept from you, Aleksandr,
> Is that you were cruel and handsome!

vii

In such knowledge, as the two citations show, the poet keeps something, which he then bestows in the poem—indeed, it is the poem which becomes the bestowal, the relinquishment of some final totality otherwise merely lost or evaded in the *private life*. We cease to be dazzled, endangered by so much experience, if we respond to the one thing the poems ask of us; for they ask of us the one thing that art must ask, not all the other things which it may: they ask of us submission. Submission to one life, then to another, picked up and put down (revealed, redeemed perhaps, in the moment's audacity of attention):

My father?
One stormy night in 1927 he rode a train in New England
While trying to memorize a poem by a Frenchman:
It said something about a mirror rising from
The sea. You know: *un miroir de la mer* . . .
Some men postpone orgasm by reciting poetry,

taken here, and then there, the perpetual *next*, at crucial ventures within the biography, at critical instances: we are always, with Dubie, upon the verge of extinction or of ecstatic renunciation, some grand romantic fantasia upon broken themes of dispossession and metamorphosis. Proust and Ovid, silver-age Russians (Blok, Babel, Mandelstam), Klee and Breughel, the deposed Czar ("I teach the children about decreasing fractions," he writes from his captivity in the Ekaterinburg barn, "that is a lesson best taught by the father"): it is always the experience which has the root of *peril* in it, the ripple of danger which enlivens the seemingly lovely surfaces, the "ordinary" existence. And as I say, Dubie identifies that experience, by reciting it, with his own life to a hallucinatory degree: we are not to know what is given and what is taken, what is "real" and what "made up." What we know is that three things can be said about all of us—that we were, that we are, and that we will not be. We listen then (no clue who is speaking) to a recital of experience with no hint of recurrence, no hope of repetition, yet not in prose even so, for there is

Dubie's rage for unity from the start and throughout, making even the most intricate and weird of his notations (mostly declarative utterance: "the bald heads of two priests can be seen / like the white buttocks of the lovers fleeing into the trees," or more tenderly:

> The water is green. The two boats out at a distance
> Are silver, and the two gulls coming in
> Off the water are, also, silver;)

round on themselves and form a whole, even if it is a whole enigma, a whole labyrinth, a mystery entire. We listen, then, in what I recommend as a posture of submission. Best to let the poet tell, in that shocking way of his, what you can see or hear by his lights, what morning looks like on the curtains, and what century it is. He is, as they say, a natural (they mean: we do not yet understand such art), and he will often be able to compel a recognition-scene from just the moments most alien to your experience: it is because he has *created* your experience in the poem, has preempted you as he has assimilated Boehme and Mme. Blavatsky, and there is no pulling apart the intestinal warp now, no mine and thine about the texture, as in this aperçu from "The Boy Breughel":

> Ice in the river begins to move,
> And a boy in a red shirt who woke
> A moment ago
> Watches from his window
> The street where an ox
> Who's broken out of his hut
> Stands in the fresh snow
> Staring cross-eyed at the boy
> Who smiles and looks out
> Across the roof to the hill;
> And the sun is reaching down
> Into the woods

Where the smoky red fox still
Eats his kill. Two colors.
Just two colors!
A sunrise. The snow.

It is because Dubie has created *your* experience by the words in his poem (his? who is "he"? Breughel? The reader? The painting?) that he obtains the submission he requires (Dubie is very chary about revealing his *other* means of obtaining it, hides his rhymes and rhythmic insistences within a hugely idiosyncratic method of enjambments, "the regalia inside"). We yield to these poems because they value our confusions, our shames.

Indeed so intimate is his scrutiny of the nostalgias, as Wallace Stevens would say, that Dubie appears unable to forget—to subordinate any experience to some other; thereby he occludes what we have agreed to call meaning (to mean is to see resemblances, repetitions), but he enlarges what we have agreed to call value (to value is to see differences, singularities). As the poet says:

And my mother pale with her red hair rests,
At midnight, looking out the kitchen window where
All summer the fat moths were knocking their
Brains out against the lamp in the henhouse,

But now the moths are replaced with large
Flakes of snow, and there's no difference, moths
Or snow, for their lives are so short
That while they live they are already historical. . . .

That you may grant this assertion—that the poem can create your experience of the world rather than that your experience must create the poem—is the risk Dubie takes, his cherished peril. He has put *himself* as medium in the service of an art which, of us, asks that submission merely. Of him it asks everything else.

Richard Howard

I

For Hannah

Some tree whose broad smooth leaves
together sewed.

PARADISE LOST IX

NINETEEN FORTY

They got Lewes at last yesterday.
VIRGINIA WOOLF

The sun just drops down through the poplars.

I should sit out and watch it rather than
Write this!

The red of it sweeps along the houses past the marsh
To where L. is picking apples.
The air is cold.
Little things seem large.
Behind me there's moisture like windows on the pears.

And then the planes going to London. Well, it's
An hour before that yet. There are cows eating grass.
There were bombs dropped on Itford hill. Yesterday,
I watched a Messerschmitt smudge out in the sky.

What is it like when the bone-shade is crushed in
On your eye. You drain. And pant. And, then, dot, dot, dot!

Walking Sunday (Natalie's Birthday) by Kingfisher pool
I saw my first hospital train. It was slow, but not ladened,
Not like a black shoebox, but like a weight pulled by
A string. And bone-shaking!
Private and heavy it cut through the yellow fields:

And a young airman with his head in his hands,
With his head in a fat, soiled bandage, moved
His good eye, and nothing else, up to the high corner
Of his window and through the cool, tinted glass watched,

I believe, as
Individual wild ducks scraped and screamed in along a marsh!

3

FEBRUARY: THE BOY BREUGHEL

The birches stand in their beggar's row:
Each poor tree
Has had its wrists nearly
Torn from the clear sleeves of bone,
These icy trees
Are hanging by their thumbs
Under a sun
That will begin to heal them soon,
Each will climb out
Of its own blue, oval mouth;
The river groans,
Two birds call out from the woods

And a fox crosses through snow
Down a hill; then, he runs,
He has overcome something white
Beside a white bush, he shakes
It twice, and as he turns
For the woods, the blood on the snow

Looks like the red fox,
At a distance, running down the hill:
A white rabbit in his mouth killed
By the fox in snow
Is killed over and over as just
Two colors, now, on a winter hill:

Two colors! Red and white. A barber's bowl!
Two colors like the peppers
In the windows
Of the town below the hill. Smoke comes
From the chimneys. Everything is still.

Ice in the river begins to move,
And a boy in a red shirt who woke
A moment ago
Watches from his window
The street where an ox
Who's broken out of his hut
Stands in the fresh snow
Staring cross-eyed at the boy
Who smiles and looks out
Across the roof to the hill;
And the sun is reaching down
Into the woods

Where the smoky red fox still
Eats his kill. Two colors.
Just two colors!
A sunrise. The snow.

THE CZAR'S LAST CHRISTMAS LETTER.
A BARN IN THE URALS:

You were never told, Mother, how old Illya was drunk
That last holiday, for five days and nights

He stumbled through Petersburg forming
A choir of mutes, he dressed them in pink ascension gowns

And, then, sold Father's Tirietz Stallion so to rent
A hall for his Christmas Recital: the audience

Was rowdy but Illya in his black robes turned on them
And gave them that look of his; the hall fell silent

And violently he threw his hair to the side and up
Went the baton, the recital ended exactly one hour

Later when Illya suddenly turned and bowed
And his mutes bowed, and what applause and hollering

Followed.
All of his cronies were there!

Illya told us later that he thought the voices
Of mutes combine in a sound

Like wind passing through big, winter pines.
Mother, if for no other reason I regret the war

With Japan for, you must now be told,
It took the servant, Illya, from us. *It was confirmed.*

He would sit on the rocks by the water and with his stiletto
Open clams and pop the raw meats into his mouth

And drool and laugh at us children.
We hear guns often, now, down near the village.

Don't think me a coward, Mother, but it is comfortable
Now that I am no longer Czar. I can take pleasure

From just a cup of clear water. I hear Illya's choir often.
I teach the children about decreasing fractions, that is

A lesson best taught by the father.
Alexandra conducts the French and singing lessons.

Mother, we are again a physical couple.
I brush out her hair for her at night.

She thinks that we'll be rowing outside Geneva
By the Spring. I hope she won't be disappointed.

Yesterday morning while bread was frying
In one corner, she in another washed all of her legs

Right in front of the children. I think
We all became sad at her beauty. She has a purple bruise

On an ankle.
Like Illya I made her chew on mint.

Our Christmas will be in this excellent barn.
The guards flirt with your granddaughters and I see . . .

I see nothing wrong in it. Your little one, who is
Now a woman, made one soldier pose for her, she did

Him in charcoal, but as a bold nude. He was
Such an obvious virgin about it; he was wonderful!

Today, that same young man found us an enormous azure
And pearl samovar. Once, he called me Great Father

And got confused.
He refused to let me touch him.

I know they keep your letters from us. But, Mother,
The day they finally put them in my hands

I'll know that possessing them I am condemned
And possibly even my wife, and my children?

We will drink mint tea this evening.
Will each of us be increased by death?

With fractions as the bottom integer gets bigger, Mother, it
Represents less. That's the feeling I have about

This letter. I am at your request, The Czar.
And I am Nicholas.

THE GREAT AMERICAN NOVEL:
WINTER, 1927

For P.S.

1.

You woke, and in the headlights you saw first
The heavy snow falling in across the pond,
Then, around the corner onto
The stone bridge up past the dark stand
Of pines to where the village slopes off
And into the night and Frederick's Notch;
Here is where your mother had her accident,
The silver-blue snout of your grandfather's
Stutz-bearcat ploughing into a snowbank:
Your mother is laughing, steps out in a pink gown

Catching the blood from her nose in a champagne glass
Which has shattered at the bottom:
There's just the long clear stem
And the bowl filling with blood; she's
There with one hand on the chauffeur's chest
And in the other this icy, dripping flower.
This red flower! Poor Marcel Proust, his
Mother put her wooden teeth out each night
In a box of salt and flour. You wrote, once,
An imaginary letter to Proust, it ended with

A piano being dragged out of the house and into
The snow, it was left under two bare trees
Until sunset. Then, it was splashed with
Gasoline and set on fire. When the first leg
Gave out the piano slumped forward
Like a painfully slow, performing elephant!
Marcel Proust loved Indian-jugglers,

9

Performing tigers and wild elephants.
Your mother and her young chauffeur in his turquoise
Trousers begin to stumble back

Down the road to the icehouse at Island-Pond.
It is just within an hour, now, that your life
Was begun; your father is on a train
In New Hampshire, next month he will die of fever
In Spain. Your mother and the chauffeur dressed
In pink and blue walk down the road keeping
Near to the woods. The snow falls around them.
And up behind them on the hill the Stutz-bearcat
Explodes, catching on fire: here and there lights
Are turned on down in the village.

By now the chauffeur has offered his flask
To your mother who nervously touches her yellow hair;
By now your mother is only bleeding at the wrist
And thumb. And there is the sound of someone sobbing!

2. THE LETTER:

Marcel: you know, *un miroir de la mer se lève* . . .
I believe I was
Conceived in an icehouse during a winter storm?
I believe they were sprawled naked on a long
Slab of ice like in a 19th Century morgue littered
With straw and sawdust. And
While on her back she just stared
Into the corner at a clear block of ice
That had inside it an orange and white dragon-fly.
Marcel, its mouth and wings were incandescent!

There was shattered glass in the corner and
Someone's blue trousers.

I believe, Marcel, you never left that room in Paris?
I visit a grave in Spain once each year.
It's a grave of a dead musician. My father?
One stormy night in 1927 he rode a train in New England
While trying to memorize a poem by a Frenchman:
It said something about a mirror rising from
The sea. You know: *un miroir de la mer* . . .
Some men postpone orgasm by reciting poetry.

My mother would sit on top of a piano and
My father would play violent parodies of Liszt
And Chopin. My mother's eyes were
Green like pond-ice, and her shoulders
Were always freckled. Her eyelids
Were blue. She hated insects.
Once, in a garden, hornets climbed out of
A hedge and sleepy like swimmers rising in water
They climbed up under her shirt which she had
Loosened in the heat. She ran stripping to the waist;

She ran in the direction of the gate. I remember
Her breasts were the color of cream
And pendulous for a woman so thin.
And, Marcel,
I know you won't answer my letters? Nevertheless . . .
They walked down the hill and there was
Blood on her slippers. They walked near to the woods.
She stumbled often. They drank his bourbon.
They are both young and it's still snowing
As they enter the icehouse. My grandfather's black

Rowboat is there and she sits down in the middle
Of it.
And by now I am there: And, Marcel, I am, also,
Incandescent like an elephant walking the savanna at sunset!

THE NEGRESS: HER MONOLOGUE OF
DARK CRÊPE WITH EDGES OF LIGHT:

Mistress Adrienne, I have been given a bed with a pink dresser
In the hot-house
Joining the Concord Public Library: the walls and roof are
Glass and my privacy comes from the apple-geraniums,
Violets, ferns, marigolds and white mayflags.
I get my meals
With the janitor and his wife and all of the books are mine
To use. I scour, sweep and dust.
I hope you don't think of me
As a runaway? I remember your kindness,
Your lessons in reading and writing on the piazza.
My journey was unusual. I saw some of the war
And it was terrible even far up into the North.
My first fright was at a train depot outside Memphis
Where some soldiers found me eating not yet ripened
Quinces and grapes, they took me prisoner: first
I helped some children carry tree limbs to the woodbox
Of the locomotive, then, I was shown to a gentleman
In the passenger car who was searching for his runaway
Negress in a purple dress; he wouldn't identify me,

And I was thrown in with about forty stray blacks into
An open boxcar and soon we were moving, next to me
A man was sucking on the small breasts of a girl
Maybe twelve years of age, across from them
A sad old woman smiled as she puffed on an old cigar end,
By afternoon she was dead, her two friends
Just kicked her out so that she rolled down into pasture
Frightening some hogs that ran off into a thicket.
The girl next to me whimpered and shook. Those quinces
Just ran straight through me and all I could do was

Squat in one corner that was supplied with ammonia-waters
And hay. We were given that night Confederate uniforms
To mend and when the others slept I dressed in three
Shirts and trousers and leapt from the moving train,
The padding helped some but I couldn't walk the next day.
I hid in a shack that seemed lonely but for a flock
Of turkeys, some young hens and a corn crib with tall
Split palings. The next morning from a hill
I watched field workers on a tobacco plantation, it took
Two men to carry a single leaf like a corpse from
A battle scene. That night I found a horse with a bit
In its mouth made of telegraph wire. He carried me up all
The way to Youngstown. *Chloe, you must*
Learn to swim in the pond and to ride the old sorrel.
I am grateful. I had to swim two rivers. I fished some
For perch, bream and trout and ate dried berries.
I stole a bushel of oysters from the porch of a farmhouse.
I treated my sores with blackgum from poplars. I witnessed
The hanging of three Confederate soldiers at a trestle:
Once they were done dancing, they settled in their greatcoats
Like dead folded birds. I have a hatred
Of men and I walked away from the trestle singing.
I spoke to The Concord Literary Club last Tuesday
About my experiences. I told them you never did
Abuse me. How we would sit out in the gazebo
And listen to the boys with their violins, tambourines,
Bones, drums and sticks. How we wept as girls
When the fox bit the head off our peahen and that
From that day how the peacock, missing his mate, would
See her in his reflection in a downstairs window
And fly at it increasing his iridescence with lacerations.

When I left you the windows were all missing and daubers
Were making their mud houses in the high corners
Of the hallway. With sugar-water and crêpe I have put a new
Hem on my purple dress.

At night I walk down the aisles
Of the library, the books climb twenty feet above me,
I just walk there naked with my tiny lamp.
I have the need to fling the lamp sometimes: but I resist it.
Mistress Adrienne, I saw three big cities burning!
Did you know ladies from Philadelphia rode for two days
In wagons to climb a hill where with spyglasses they watched
The war like a horse-pulling contest at a fair.
The man beside me on the train who was sucking the little
Girl's breasts, he was your stable boy, Napoleon. He said
He never had a bad word for you. His little mistress was
Still bare to the waist and before I leapt from the train,
And while he slept, I ran a rod into his eye. I stabbed him
In his brain. She stopped weeping.
Remember that French lullaby where two fleas in a gentleman's
Moustache die like a kiss between the lips of the gentleman
And his mistress. How we laughed at it!
I hope you were not long unconscious there beside the pond.
I just ran away from you, listening the whole night
For your father's hounds. I am
Afraid I split your parasol on your skull. If I
Don't hear from you I will try to understand. *Chloe*.

THE UGLY POEM THAT RELUCTANTLY
ACCEPTS *ITSELF* AS ITS ONLY TITLE:

For Weingarten

It's that icy, blue, chain-dragging sincerity of ghosts just
Screaming out under the linden tree in a book
Written before Lincoln was born; and it's

Abraham Lincoln who slept alone and better than his wife did.
He was once being entertained by a prince
Who had brought as a gift his celebrated mongoose, *Keise*:
At first, the ochre and red eyes of the mongoose were closed;
He seemed wounded, and the snake swayed back,
At that instant, the mongoose sunk his teeth
Into the soft mauve jewel on the cobra's hood. The snake
Straightened like a wave, Lincoln said!

John Wilkes Booth thought sex was a preparation for death,
You read that letter of his to me in your farmhouse
By the creek in the steamy Iowa landscape:
                                        remember the morning
By the railway depot where Lincoln had once waved
To the black-and-lavender Amish children: beside
That depot we watched an Angus bull that suddenly stood,
Balancing on the spotted rump of a young cow,
A huge violet artery crossed his square face, he sniffed
The air and looked with downcast eyes from the fields
To the willow trees that ran beside the river;
The cow cried out and the towering Angus bellowed back at her,
And the cow, then, looked
Over herself to the bull who was just finishing: large flies,

As in Tier's photographs of the dead in the South, were walking
Across his open eyes and into his nostrils and mouth!

THESE UNTITLED LITTLE VERSES
IN WHICH, AT DAWN, TWO OBSCURE
DUTCH PEASANTS STRUGGLED WITH
AN AUBURN HORSE:

after *a painting by Willem van de Velde. The Elder.*

The water is green. The two boats out at a distance
Are silver, and the two gulls coming in

Off the water are, also, silver;
But these peasants and their horse, at first light,

Seem absorbed in the pitch-blackness
Of a previous night. They are in a field

That climbs away from the sea joining
A thick row of white almond trees.

The younger of the two men holds a small branch,
The other

Holds a rope that leads away from the horse
Running over his shoulder and underneath the arm

To a pool of rope beneath him: he leans,
Or he reclines like a lever in the scene.

The auburn horse
Represents some inevitable sadness

That will visit each of us, that visits
These two peasants struggling in a winter pasture.

It is the morning.
It is dawn. These three may

16

Signal a common enough passage from the night
To the day. It begins like pain for the older man:

It begins to rain.
The two men run to the trees just above them

And the horse, ignorant of everything, walks away
Like a skilled butcher from a dark, maimed

Lamb still wiggling in the grass behind him. And
Morning surrenders to mid-day, and the afternoon

To the evening, and the evening surrenders everything
To the sleep of these two peasants

Who have had a discouraging day in the fields:
They dream of the black, burial horses of a king

With heavy sable plumes and the blinders
Of gold-leaf made starry with diamonds,

Horses not like the auburn mare who stood
In a world that

Belongs to a system of things
Which presents a dark humus with everything

Living: all of us preceded
Not by the lovely, braided horses

Of which the peasants dreamed, but by these two
Peasants and their horse struggling

Briefly, at dawn, in the deep trenches
Of a field beside the green, winter sea!

WAR AND PEACE

For Michael Burkard

I've defended you against nothing the entire night.
Now, put wood under your cot and I'll light it.
There are recruits and two barbers standing
In the river. Shaves and haircuts. A straw hat.
Lean into it with a resemblance of singing
And be glad. But, Mishka, who put the twigs
In the pickle water with centuries of weather
Ahead of us? There were people with lanterns
Appearing at the windows. And a young lieutenant
Eating a raw potato while thinking of his wife's
Apartments in Moscow.

It's at times like these that you think
You are not dead. When you are most alive
And your friends ahead of you are naked
And scratching their backs with tree branches.
Everyone would say they are thinking
Of women. But what happens next is much different
Like throwing eggs at a prisoner who chooses
To describe the end of happiness in winter
As the beginning of something like his daughter
Being lowered into a tub of ice water
And you think then that it is not a matter of
A smelly fox in the middle of a forest. But that
Was what he told her.

THE RED PADRONA FOR JOSÉ CUEVAS

Just moving ad lib *on foot, horse or motorcar across
deserts and through canyons . . . this is just a life
outside, and the outside of life. Not really life, in my
opinion. . . . But Frieda loves it.*
FROM THE LETTERS OF D. H. LAWRENCE.

Frieda is sitting on a pony beside a twisted smoke-tree.
She is dressed in an open blue shirt.
Her long arms are red.
The flowering sage and creosote behind her

Are yellow and silver. And the darkness between them,
Between her and the flowers, isn't
A cloudburst off in the distance, but a field of alfalfa.
This is the desert at night.

Behind the woman there's a railway station,
A giant cactus and the moon.

You can hear the doves snoring in their stick nests.
In the morning the sun will touch their new eggs,
All latitude and white-hot, the spaces between the eggs
Are filled with cow hair and parts of dry mice.

This woman on the pony is the wife of the painter
Who in silver and mustard paints the adobe cubes
Of the pueblo that rise, now, behind her, unlikely
But used as the night.

The widows of the pueblo sing
To the Kingbirds and the Black Phoebes.
In the morning the wrens hurl
Themselves at these women
Who walk to the artesian tank
With dusty cattle following slowly behind them.

19

The woman on the pony is dressed in an open blue shirt.
Her long arms are red.
Frieda is a widow.
Here, in the desert *once* is *always*, and memory
Like the summer is white-hot, but complicated.
The siesta is complicated because it rivals

The wife.

The flowering sage and creosote behind her
Are yellow and silver. And the darkness between them,
Between her and the flowers, isn't
Rain off in the distance, it's a creation
Of her husband's, made in the perspective
Of the desert
Where her evenings and mornings are not separate. *Again,*

Frieda is a subject.

She is the woman on a gray pony beside a smoke-tree.
In the distance she can hear a bell
Rattling up in the white tower of a mission.
She is patient with her husband
Who is painting her as a simple figure outside, at night,
In the desert:

And if you imagine she is being watched, then
She will never be lonely
As much later under a street lamp in London:
She nervously revolves a parasol above her, and
The orbs and tassels on the parasol rise and fall,
Musical somehow

Like heavy blue buzzards in the air above a lame burro.

THE WEDDING PARTY

When the large frame of the window collapses in the fire
It's like a huge woman
With her hands on her hips, the bones below her waist
Spread with leaves, about to strike
A frail child and the bones of his face
Spread with more leaves, two
Bowls slapped with mud and baked with everyone outside
Screaming in the smoke in the hall where she waltzed
Away, she thought, with the sergeant.

There are phrases like cold fish, or a triangle balanced
On the nose of another triangle. The woman in a formal gown
Tossed out on the snow, a black leg and her husband draped
Over the table with his hand in the punch bowl. The daughter
Was near the folded chair in the middle of the wall.

But don't stop; cross the room and follow those people
Just coming in; go down the stairs
Leading to the toilets;
Open the door in front of you; the small cellar
With the window kicked out. It will all come down
To this level. The barrel-organs, the hat that collected
The printed invitations, the conductor, the vows
And the bean flower the bride had grown for her father.

These are not the memories of a country wedding.
The one bird brought inside appears outside
And will not be interviewed.
Even the amateurs who moved the piano
Have gone aside with their sandwiches. Their boss takes
Off his spectacles, lays them down, gazes beyond
It all at some addition to the moon. You must look

At her as well. He decides whether or not to take off
His hat. To drink? *Can you hear me? Just yes or no.*

The women huddled on the roof far away are disappointed;
The thrill, the calamity, was over.
Hadn't it just started? They hug their blankets.
One by one they climb down the ladder in boredom.
Getting into bed the second time within
Two hours is a dilemma not like dying in a fire after
The wedding. And
In the extreme heat the tuba in the corner took on
A new curl. In the morning a small boy blows into it.
A drunk lying out in the trees hears him,
All the false starts, nothing like it in the world. The music
Telling him to get up and walk away. But first he searches
For the hat that he wore to a wedding.

THE IMMORALIST

Samaden, the Julier, Tiefenkasten . . . the raw egg
I broke into the harness bells, and the strong reversals
Of cold, sour wine. The marshlike waters on the other
Honeymoon were a new train, as early as Neuchâtel, and
Overlooking a lake, past some cows, the first signals
Of melancholy. I didn't leave her all day.

I had heard of other cases of tuberculosis
That were much worse. And wasn't there something
I didn't know about myself? I blamed everything on
Whatever few biscuits Marceline broke
Into her soup. She coughed horribly.
Besides, what did we need money for? A winter in Engadine?
I no longer have my lectures. We are drunk and weak.

I have again made love to a woman saving blood
In her mouth. I remember the way the other sloshed
Wine around with her tongue. Her laughter.
And the reeds of a hideous black lake. The hotel
Was empty. The honest Swiss. Even their rosebushes
Told her I would push a pillow
To her face. (Hard benches by the water, and the blankets
Over her legs. I didn't leave her all day.)

From the train through glass: larches and fir,
And the crease of the pillowcase on her black cheek
Filling slowly like her grave,
Like the trench of a young couple crossing a lake.

FOR OSIP MANDELSTAM

Almost a century ago eleven mousetraps
Were set out in large houses in Prague,
Until now the mice, these iron traps and
The houses have been ignored, yet tonight
My wife asleep will hear the unlocking,
The sentimentality of some necks breaking, and
Will see eleven old women climbing stairs,
With dustpans, their stockings
Falling down, reaching the forgotten
Traps to sweep them clean of everything
That was alive in her memory
And, until now, just inside the walls.

And I hate every last one of you
Who reads this silently or aloud
For being in the next apartment
With your ears against our wall.
You heard her weeping?
You think her breasts are like marble with
A large blue vein standing out. You were
Our friends, and in the yellow evenings
She walks through your rooms
Watering your blank flowers for you.

Your scratching is now
The noise of something just inside the walls.

THE TUB. 1934. HALIFAX, MISSISSIPPI

If a man stands by a pin oak emptying
A thermos onto the ground and it is cold
In the light, and the light itself
Has condensed
Inside his bones, would you walk up to him
And say, "I went to the clay house. It still
Smells of the hickory, even now in November.
I want to know what is going
To happen to everyone."
The sound of churchbells comes out of
The cane-brake.
The insides of three birds are smoking
On the ground by his feet. He watches

A leaf come all the way down out
Of its tree. Then he speaks, "Look, little pigeon,
What are you doing
Out here in your nightgown? Your hair
Is wet. You're standing in your bare feet
Like the girls down in the cabins.
You should have visited me earlier: I waited
For you here each evening in the summer. I covered
The bird entrails with leaves.
There was a smell of plums. The fox
Was in the clearing. Does your mother
Forgive me. I didn't mean to . . . you tell

Me 'that's lost' and 'that's dead'
And 'I don't remember ever owning a red dress.'
You know that night before I went into
The fields, as much as she had hurt me in the afternoon,
I laid down the gun

To draw water in the tub for her. She should
Find that a pleasant memory.

Tell her they were wrong. 'It could have been
An accident.'
When I went out the door the tub
Was still filling and she called to me
That she'd see to it. I have a memory of her, naked
Running to a tub as if to someone, and
Her mouth is opening. She kneels almost
Without getting near it, and, out of breath,
Just stares at the faucets for a moment; then reaches
Touching the collar of the coat. I am bleeding.
Leaves are stuck to my chest. Then, there's
A sound she hears down in the cane, and
Really it's much more
Than a sound, but not yet a noise.

It's like a tub overflowing onto a floor."

SUN AND MOON FLOWERS:
PAUL KLEE, 1879–1940

First, there is the memory of the dead priest in Norway
Dressed in a straw hat, his tie that's white
But splashed with violet and the black skirt;
He'll hang forever in the deer park.
Beneath him German officers
Are weaving in and out of trees in a white sunlight.

When there is music crossing over the water from France
The little steamers pull their beds of coal
Slowly up the canal, and, Klee,
You walk back to your room saying:
What on earth happened to us? Any simple loss
Is like the loss of all of us. Nothing's secret?
Just look straight into the North Sea.
And, then, tell me there's anything they can keep from us.

The matron who walked you through the orchard at Orsolina
Should have said: There's a black star with conifers.
Klee, don't listen to them. Next Wednesday your heart
Stops like a toad. You're dying of a skin disease.
They are not telling you about this war, the Luftwaffe,
The Nazi who's resting on a sofa beside a stream,
And, Klee, this Nazi is inside Poland. And
In Poland your moon flowers have already begun growing!

The opaque dice in your painting can no longer
Be mistaken for some weathered houses by the coast.
The woman sick with tuberculosis says to you,
"A war will clear the air!"
The war puts priests in trees. Puts a sparrow's nest
Beside a sleeve in a train station in Tuscany.

You and your friends saw the unlikely, ruptured ceilings
And painted them; but not as premonitions, or images

Of war—
The war your family won't acknowledge or discuss
But an orderly who has news of Poland whispers
To the day nurse: she touches her blouse.
You ask her what is happening.
You make a scene. And then she says what is necessary
By slipping you a morning tray

With its ice water, blue spikes of lupine, and morphine.

THE FIRST SENTENCE IS
FOR THE DEAD EIDER DUCK:

Would you like to know the key to the epoch?
OSIP MANDELSTAM

In the mist outside the glass railway station
In Pavlovsk a man sits in a heavy coat
With his collar up and smokes, and smokes:

Through the window in the barbershop

There's a single light burning, it reveals the towels,
A mug and brush and the narrow copper picture, *Coq*;
A conductor in the shadows finishes a cigar while

The man in the heavy coat listens

For the familiar popping sound of the kerosene
Street-lamps: he remembers the bone-shaking
Howitzers and two children stuffing

A white puppy inside the stomach of a horse for warmth.

A circus from Finland was attacked near here:
The mob having not eaten in a week
Slaughtered the dancing bears for meat.

A woman was seen running through the snow

With the torso of a dead cub still wearing a turquoise coat.
The trainer of the bears sat against the wall sobbing
With his broken beer stein pushed down on his head like

A crown.

Near his eye there is a trickle of blood.
Two versts away
His wife with an axe chops

At the benches in the pine groves.

The man at the glass railway station in Pavlovsk
Crushes out a cigarette with his boot
And stands in the winter fog: he has memorized

A poem in which a brown naked girl with an ikon-lamp

Enters a bedroom: her hair reaches
Down her back and the little blue flame
Inside the ikon is like a dusty grape

In the beak of a raven.

This dark woman is his wife as a girl
And she is in Moscow boiling rabbit blood, now,
And running it through scarves onto flour

For paste she'll eat on dark bread until Wednesday.

There's white fur under her fingernails. She floats
Dead coals in her water pail so it won't
Spill as she hurries through the cold.

She is withered with a fox-like chin. She stomps

Her foot hearing mazurkas falling away
To a single despondent violin.
It is silent in her apartment; but for her foot

That's merciless like a rifle-butt pulverizing
                    the spud-like nose of a bear cub.

AFRICA

I expand my chest for the children.

There are no longer the floors
That are ceilings. There is the stone room;
And in the center of the room
I train gladiators, the breeze
From their iron nets releasing me
From all guilt
For what I am about to say:

(The lion crosses the arena and leaps;
From underneath you are shocked
With his yellow chest, the darker
Hairs like the silhouette of your
Daughter you wore as a medal,
Through two wars, around your neck.

The ragged bronze of the spearhead
Enters at this target.) She carries
A basin of water out to you. The cheering.
You look up at her and say, "but
This cat and you are dead, I've just
Killed you both, twice, in resemblance."

(The last granary of Rome, the woodlands
Becoming savanna, iroko and tree ferns,
And the jungle with its
Low deciduous understory
Which the legions burn. In chains
From Walvis Bay to Mocâmedes.)

A cold sponge touches your eyebrows.

On the coast in the wet huts your daughter
Is still alive
Making picture books: the zigzag lines, her ladders,
And the chest of the dead cat, yellow and red
Like the night horizon.

HORACE

Along the borders of the Sabine farm,
Runners of strychnine and lime,
A bearded man stands in a wheelbarrow
Singing. And why not? Give him
The vegetables he wants.
Or knock his brains out with the loose
Curbstone from the well. The Goths
Have been defeated, and Maecenas was his friend.

We meet eye to eye. He will braid the silk
On the husks. This man is drunk.
The cloudburst sends you running for the trees
And one woman reaches the house. He is still
Standing in the wheelbarrow, soaked and loud.
The poor canvas theatre in the provincial town
Drove him out. Here in the hills
Caesar is a spectacle of dead trout
Washed with smashed mint and lemons.
What have I kept back?
Only this: there is no way to leave him.

IBIS:

For Lorry Goldensohn

There is the long dream in the afternoon
That turns a large, white page

Like, once, the slow movement
Of slaves at daybreak

Through the clouds of a stone laundry.
The blossom

On a black vegetable and
The olive wood burning in the plate

Are the simple events
That I'll wake to this evening.

At dark, we'll walk out along
The shore having finished

Another day of exile in a wet place.
As a boy I burned

Leaves in the many gardens
Of a cemetery in Rome.

I wrote in my diary:
A blue vessel

Is filling out in the rain. All day,
Here, the water falls and is not broken,

But it punishes me like the girls
With their clubs and bowl

Flattening the new maize,
Millet, and the narrow tubers

Of yam
That are white like hill snow.

Postumius is my servant-boy, he plays
All morning in the sea.

He says, "Ovid. The red ibis flies north!"
I hate him.

He visits me between phantoms
And like them,

Like the goat, you can trace the muscles
In his leg and the purple ropes

Of blood that climb
Through his throat. At the salt-marsh

He searches for the moon snail
With its lavender egg-pouch;

He eats them after
Soaking them in brookwater . . .

Days that follow in rain
Make him nervous and he eats

Everything off the dry shelf: the individual
Oval seeds, he cracks

The winter wheat between his teeth
With a sound

Like a child working its teeth
In a bad dream.

If he stands all day in the marsh
In the sun, then, he returns to me

As a new coin. I am jealous
Of him.

He smiles at me. There are the shadows
With the olive wood burning in the plate.

It's dark. We walk out along
The shore of the Black Sea.

There's the noise of the ibis
Who raises a bleached wing in waking.

There is a boat decaying by a tree.
It's radiant

Like the shearwater birds
Standing here and there among rocks.

Postumius touches my shoulder, "Ovid?
About Rome when the moon

Was broken on the ground and the ferns
Stood against the blue-black sky?"

I do remember the bleachers in the arena
And a lion's paw raised, that erased

The face of a young Thracian.
I tell him he is a stupid boy!

We walk back
Passing the wharves and straw-houses.

I say to Postumius
That when I am dead

He must fuel the terracotta lamp
And gather the cress and hidden eggs

Of the ibis. He smiles at me, I do
Love him, at moments;

As, then, he sleeps next to me,
Never sharing the work

Of turning the page, as slowly he turns
All of his new body away from me.

II

ELEGIES FOR THE OCHRE DEER
ON THE WALLS AT LASCAUX

For Harold Alenius, 1913–1959

This and the like together establish the realm of *It.*

"In order to come to love," says Kierkegaard about his renunciation of Regina Olsen, "I had to remove the object."

Kierkegaard does not conceal from us for a moment that his religious doctrine of loneliness is personal. He confesses that he "ceased to have common speech" with men. He notes that the finest moment in his life is in the bath house, before he plunges into the water: "by then I am having nothing more to do with the world."

MARTIN BUBER

PROLOGUE

You are hearing a distant, almost familiar, French cradle-song
While drinking bottled water
Along the roadside to Copenhagen.

There are children of six who speak
In secret to imaginary friends
On summer evenings before bed.

In some old houses there are walls where there were doors.
And doors where there were windows.
And where there were once floors of broken field stones
There are, now, blue ceilings.

There is a sudden smell of roses in a room.

Once, there was a hunter
Dressed in skins, in the black and mauve summer-molt of bison,
And he would squat down before a wet, serpentine wall and make

An image. (A virgin is singing: My Lords, turn in, turn in!)

I suppose all of this means nothing to you; there's still
The blue tiles of the bath house floor, and the orange lamps
Burning above the moving surface of the water. A nude lawyer
Is smoking a cigar on a birch-sofa next to a lieutenant
Who's exercising in an Army blanket. You'll forget them
As you leave the edge making a little figure
In the air as you enter the steaming, blue pool:

Søren, a winter evening in the bath house, and just past
The surface of the water you saw

The *will to be*!

The *will to be* is, perhaps, teeth, throat
And intestine leaving the floor of an ocean just
With the slight movement of its tail. The *will to be* is often
Not pretty, but dorsal like the sable plumes on helmets, or

Like the man at Lascaux in his black and mauve skins
Who with friends stands at the edge of a pit
That holds reindeer, they shower the deer with stones,
And, then, suddenly there's a silence: our caveman

Reaches down into the pit and draws out a white fawn
Who, weak from swimming in the blood of the others, wobbles
For a moment and, then, runs off into a forest: *and, Søren,*

The fawn made bright, finite tracks through the leaves
Like your own red lettering in a diary

That believes the gods of China must be Chinese!

1. 1916

The way the mist in the mountains can circle a young fir,
A boulder or the fern and purple vetch of the timberline
Which are waving as children after a pageant
Through the mist and rain to someone seated way above them
On a rotting bench at the summit of the mountain.
It's young Theodisius, the Jesuit,

Breathing heavily
After his climb, remembering a formal procession
Up a hill in St. Louis. He looks down through the Notch:

The priest knows desire to be a comedy of place and
A surge forward as with the boy and his tuba
In this parade at St. Louis: the boy had become faint
In his blue wool suit and silver cap,
And so under the sun while descending the hill he suddenly
Went rudely through ranks of clarinets and, then,
He wrecked a section of oboes and bassoons:

Death is a descent, or the traverse that is like
A surprising destruction of music moving
With the force of a sun-struck tuba
Down a hill where, at last, our fainting musician falls
Into the arms of laughing women
Who are wearing large hats and red pantaloons.

Theodisius is romantic; he has climbed a mountain
In the mist and rain to wait, now, through the day
For a change in the weather, for the sun to burn through
And what joy he'll feel

At the ease with which individual trees

Are regained in a familiar enough
Landscape of mountains with a clear lake and ponds.

In China, Theodisius would be mistaken for an eccentric,

But a conventional Chinese wisdom has always taken
The musician in his green trout-gown for being
Eccentric as he is musical.
Theodisius' instrument was the tuba.

Yes, our Jesuit often thinks of concepts of death
When reminded of childhood embarrassments.
Theodisius is a young Jesuit who remembers
The sad little crèche in Bethlehem.

He is now waiting for the sun to burn away the mist
In the mountains: *the beer-gardens of St. Louis were often
Like this*. Anyway,

The fern and purple vetch are waving to the young priest
Who leaves his wet bench like Odysseus climbing up
Out of the surf: it's early morning,
He stares to the East where he thinks the sun will soon
Break everything wide open:

Theodisius, our poor Theodisius, still stands in mist.

He studies the cascades and a flaw in an icy waterfall,
He remembers
How his mother each Spring boiled her best crystal chandelier
Through the long hours of the afternoon into evening.
Theodisius believes that beyond all doubt he is dangerous
To himself.

There have been many changes in him, and none
In the weather: he remembers
His mother's playing cards that were perfumed with balsam,
And how confidently she flicked them out singly

Over the table, how the young men seated
At the table could not remove their eyes
From her quick hands or her exposed bosom just beyond them.

Once crossing a stream with her, here, in these mountains
She lifted her skirts like the women in the lithograph
Of a circus at Trieste,
And Theodisius, a boy of twelve, went face first
Into the water, his mother laughing as she joined him:

They are both laughing now as they embrace,
Suspended, not quite seated on the stream bed.
Theodisius thought all the colors of that lithograph
Were there in that water. He forgets,

And looks down into the spruce and aspen.
He spots several deer along the edges of a clearing.
He approaches them like a man
Falling through crust in a snowfield.
He is still thinking of his mother; this time, as she leans
Smiling over a balcony beside a white tree.
He thought the skin of the deer seemed shaded
As with lichen. The deer knew he was weak.
But they clattered off over the stone surface of the clearing
Into the mist and leaves.
Theodisius looked away from them to the running stream
With its small delays: the silver archipelagoes,

43

Pools and blue basins.
He remembered Greek girls dancing in the beer-gardens
Of St. Louis.

Deserted even by the gentle deer, Theodisius

Became monumental and literal: he believed
He was just the breeze tipping a wet bough of a tree, a breeze
Created by the passing of a red caboose pulled along swiftly
Over a mountain trellis,

A mountain trellis which stands in the sudden sunlight
Just beneath him, the mountain trellis
From which he hangs by the neck like the pastel daredevil
At Trieste in a famous lithograph
His mother nailed to the headboard of his small bed

Just beneath a chartreuse and red watercolor of the dead Jesus.

2. 1872

Isiah Potter walks solemnly from his old salt-box
And tar-shingle house onto the stone walk
And looks up the street past the roses
To the granite hitching-posts. He loves the Orient.

Reverend Potter is composing a sermon
On the tragedy of green. He walks down the street
Under the elms thinking that once in a vision
He saw two men mowing in a field: there were ashes
On their shoulders and long daffodils shot through
Their necks and chests like arrows: he heard

An isolated choir up in a stand of trees
Behind the field. He woke, it was midnight
And he went down to the kitchen for bread in milk.
His father, Amos,
Had been dead for two winters. All the new moons
And sabbaths. The grief calling of women and children.
Isiah Potter killed himself by leaping
From a ledge into the lake. The village wanted
A dull lighting of his face, a green abscissa
In his memory, in the vestibule of the meeting house.
The portrait of Isiah Potter has remained
In the vestibule for a hundred years, and

The nighthawks are still crying above the ledges of the lake,
And below them on the rocks a young raccoon
Who's just eaten a sunfish washes his paws
And legs; he looks up at the nightsky where

Suddenly there is something like sheet-lightning
Giving way to the yellow, blue and pink parachutes

Of The Chinese Fire & Rain which is spreading out
Over the lake and dissolving back into a white light,
And, again, it's the arsenic and antimony
Of The Snow Orchard: this is fireworks

Streaming steadily, now, from two large wooden boats
That were rowed quietly to the middle of the lake.

There's the shooting sparks of The Blue Fox,
The Snow Orchard, again, but mixed with two rockets
Of gold Cassandra Buttons, and, then, after a silence
Where the frogs begin once more with their groaning:
There's the explosion of a loud, red Camphor Goose.

There's the smell of gunpowder. You can hear the water
Coming up against the rocks and trees along the shore.
And the spotted animals in the leaves have begun breathing,
For centuries in China the sky was painted on moonless nights;
What did the civet cats, martens and black bear of Liaosi Lake
Do watching soldiers with torches touching
Off rockets beside an old pavillion of wet, banyan leaves:

The white Calomel Fountain goes up blazing with the low fire
Of three Blue Suns, and you can make out
The terraced hillside with the tallow and yew trees,
Pine and willow, and the orange brick pagoda by a stream
Where two priests are eating melons and roots.

There was an owl in the yew tree: his eyes like twin lakes,
And the two large wooden boats are now being rowed back
To the beach where the children are letting go
Of their mothers' dresses, where watermelons

Are divided by a long, curved blade and night bathers
Are drying in the cold in the light of two fires.
A girl sits on a log

And closes her eyes wanting to see again the blues and yellows,
The falling chains of The Chinese Fire & Rain;
Her older sister is far up the beach past the rocks
And she is nude after swimming with a friend, he drags
a day-lily over her stomach and she shuts her eyes.
She, also, sees the ghostly paper chains
Falling out of the black sky into the water. She kisses

Her friend and quickly they run into the trees,
And as with the fireworks, the image
Of their white buttocks stays behind in the mind
Of a young raccoon who's on the rocks trembling,
The dark circles around his eyes are increasingly
Larger like the circles of broken water
On the lake where a fish has just jumped for a deerfly:

This, then, was midsummer, not a new season:

It's Isiah Potter's sermon about the green tips
Of things, a green conclusion to everything.
Accept death, he says, don't fear the daffodils
That pierce your chest or the ones that are burning
As they arc through the open windows of your houses.

Isiah Potter walked solemnly from his old salt-box
And tar-shingle house onto a stone walk
And looked up the street past the roses
To the Orient. (He woke a lunatic.) It was

The Sabbath, and he worked on his sermon
As he walked toward the meetinghouse: the green things,

The judgments and the faintings in the first garden
In the gilded book, the monotony of an animal or angel,
The couple nude beside the rocks, and

He thought: the eyes of the owl are twin, green lakes
As it glides down from its tree in China, closing, now,
On a fieldmouse where suddenly there are four rockets

Climbing: a white fountain and three blue suns burning
And the owl crumpled on the terraced hillside. Also,

He thought,
The bald heads of two priests can be seen
Like the white buttocks of the lovers fleeing into the trees.

The old woman is on her side on the sofa: the vase
Beside her is a fountain of red straw.
The old woman
Has been dead for some time now.

She drank her tea and stretched out on the sofa.
She looked out the open window
Across the street to where under the trees
The local orchestra was beginning something small
By Debussy. She watched a boy
Lift his tuba off the grass.
And with his first clear note she began to chill;
Her eyes never closed. She was just there
In her purple dress on the sofa. And
Through the open window all that night the boy
With the tuba was watched as if by an animal
Or monarch. You know how passengers

On a train prepare themselves
For a tunnel: they are watching the fir trees
That darken the hillsides while, separate and shy,
They begin to enter a mountain, they straighten
Under the white ropes and cool purple curtains:
There's a fat woman
Over there who neglects her lap-dog and looks
As if she was stabbed in the neck, the banker
Beside you was maybe kicked by a horse in the head
And even the child across from you
Stops sucking on her mother's breast and looks up
Having swallowed perhaps a coin or hatpin.

The victims of composition as dead passengers

On a train each secretly positioned
For a dark passage through rock where the ochre deer
Stand frozen, where everyone stops talking

To watch like the old woman on the sofa
Staring past her open window for a week, wanting
Very much to be discovered, she looks almost alive
Like the elephant gone perfectly still
In the mountain pass after hearing a train rush
By below him; he sniffs the air
And glances down into a forest where like him
Everything alive had stopped moving for a moment.
The train went by. The local orchestra sits
In its folding chairs and sips away at sherry,
All of them that is
But the boy with a tuba who looks
Across the street to an open window and further even

Into the dark house
Where nothing has moved for hours, where
You'll hear a voice that's not enough,
That speaks to us under the trees
Just before the white baton

Flies up:
What it says might be read aloud to children:

Tell me about the woman of many turns
Who had her tables cleaned with sponges
Who walked the beach like a motionless
Moving elephant
And who talked to the hyacinth, gull and ant.

Tell me about the woman of many turns.

And tell me you can't . . .

Only if it had been a rainy morning
There wouldn't have been
The freshly cut flowers in the hall,
Or in the garden in the sun
The small toad wouldn't have thought her straw hat
Was a second sun that had cooled
Like everything else around her.
Only if it had rained along the coast
All that morning outside her open window.
If she wasn't in the garden in the morning
She would have been alive to see
The silver tuba like a snail
Returned to the grass after the concert.

The butterfly buttons its shirt twice
In the afternoon. After working
All morning in the garden she walked
Down to the ocean and looked across to France

Where the ochre deer have stood motionless
On the cave walls for centuries.
To the hyacinth she speaks French. She doesn't
Speak to us at all. This collector of black tea:
Souchong and Orange Pekoe brewed with the seeds
Of the St. Ignatius' bean, swallowed hurriedly
In the shade of a little country parlor. *She doesn't*

Speak to us at all.

Does the barbarian cutting the throat
Of a speckled doe in China ever enjoy his solitude?
Perhaps, he's always been alone
Like the corpse dressed in purple on the sofa.
They were both strong.
They have both eaten venison.
Their venison is historical and ochre.

How do we remember them? Let me
Tell you about this woman
Who's resting on the sofa
Like a fawn fading into leaves and rocks.
She's positioned for entering

A tunnel, and, yet, for her it was just
An open window through which a boy
Reaches out for his tuba smiling

Like the Hun
Who's charging through the Empress Dowager's
Gardens, leaning down
From his horse he grabs a virgin by the hair
And lifts her off the grass

And having seen enough, this ordinary old woman
Saw an end to her suffering. *And, then,*

A white baton flew up!

THE TREES OF MADAME BLAVATSKY

There is always the cough. In the afternoon
They go out for long walks as partners,
Arms linked, woman and woman,
Man and man, woman and man. And they keep
Their feet. I can't judge if she supports
The other in green?
Perhaps, they support one another? I've
Followed them for miles and they conceal
Everything in weakness. They have
The hind legs of cows.
When horses eat fermented hay it brings up
The lining of the intestine which they
Tug at
Like gloves all the way past the elbows.

If we could follow them far enough we would
Come to their meeting place
Where they are all wired up like flowers,
They live in this camp, serene and delayed.
They are the oldest sopranos resuming
With care the phrases,
Listen, there is a song they sing at night,
The regalia inside their chests, and this song,
Which blames the memory, is wrong and not wrong
Like a girl
Showing her breasts to a boy in a cemetery.

THE MOTHS

For my mother

1. CIRCA 1582

The peninsula seen from the hills near Bath
Was a sullen black orchis, its back almost broken,
And a wooden ship once went down the river
And sat just past the headwaters at Popham,

And men, women with children, dopper birds, cows
And sheep walked out onto the sand,
Behind them the topsheets and sails were collapsing:
A great foresail followed by the mizzen skysail

And the clew moving with the mainsail
And the mizzen-royal dropping with the wet spanker.
These settlers with coughing and diarrhea
Just walked across the beach into the woods.

They made a clearing where moose would come
To eat pole-beans and lettuce.
Protestant carpenters making windowframes; and
By winter, sucking on salep and safflower, they will

Be rubbing coffins with the gestures of skaters.
A girl looks out through the trees
Remembering her fen-runners, the wax shoes
Used as skates when the grey, low-country moors were

Frozen. She remembers how the tiny oaks were silver
And blue in the snow; she'll soon be a pale, steaming
Nude in the outer lodge beside the pines
And she'll be mostly blue except for the red sores.

The Smiths, Hamels and the Ewbanks returned
To the ship in February
And the rest of their company were left in the lodge
Unburied to spindle and fray in the first hot days

Of April. Just Littre's-glands, coughing and diarrhea:
All through March the survivors would walk
Out along the deck and every so often there was a quick
Twist of the neck, a nervous look at the beach

Where ghosts appeared like a crazy, pearl bobbin jumping
On a nail of bone.
They remembered the green manure in their barns. Their
Dead were imagined in this fen-landscape.

Luke's cheeks were like two steady roses!
The wind stopped, and the river gave up the boat
Like a ghost with its topsails, studding sails and clews.
At first the woods smelled bad like an old shoe.

But then large gulls began appearing at windows
In the outer lodge, and Lewis Hamel's magnifying-glass
Drew through it sunlight, and the straw and sulphur
Smoked, the flames consumed everything nearly down to

The old gardens. They had buried their dead with fire
While they were crossing the water:
The reality of wilderness as elopement
Like believing someone is most in when there is just

An empty bed and the orchard ladder reaching to
The window; then, finding her gone they say she's dead

When she's most alive, a new bride by morning. The girl
In the lodge had blotches on her cheeks like moths,

These are her mother's fingerprints left as she touched
Her daughter last, and the icy moths
Are also like some soft fossil of a shell
You might discover out walking in the woods

Where, once, there was a peaceful, tropical ocean.

2. CIRCA 1952

(Indians stood on a hill in Bath and watched
The woods burn all afternoon, the dark smoke
Rising from the very point of the peninsula.
They believe that if you know everything

About your past you had better also know
The present moment; the risk
Isn't that you'll live in the past,
But *there* and in a future

That repeats the past. For the first time
In my life I am happy and
Living here in a desert. The palms
And lime trees have a fragrance in November

That I describe for friends in letters.
After twenty years I can now describe
The peninsula, how in April they could finally
Break the ground, and I went to Popham Village

With my father and there would be a half-dozen
Open graves and the fishermen and farmers
Who died in the winter were brought out of the Stone
House and put in the ground. Just

My father and I, a deacon and the diggers.
Hearing the prayer repeated I'd forget and
Look out at the water and watch Morris Cobb
In his rowboat checking his lobster-traps in the cove:

He is orderly like my father, now, moving from hole
To hole and, then,
I would realize his voice had fallen,
And my father moved in his robes, choking

As he moved.) While other children wondered
What happened to the dead I would
Wonder what they did with the dirt
That a coffin displaces.

When the father dies you follow him to the grave
And then walk away without him. I followed my father
To the edge but then walked back with him
Talking about something unimportant. We learn

From pilgrims raising their great beige mainsail,
The mizzen-royal and the hard slamming clews.
They practically flew away in their wooden boat.
Ghostly, they put their backs to ghosts.

The iron buckles and sleeves on a sail look
Like the dead orange fronds

Up in the palm trees. The ground snails
Falling out of the palms when it rains are

An interior weather like rain
Mixed with ice up and down the coast, and my mother
And I bringing in the wash from outside
With everything gone stiff like boards.

She was a nurse on a surgical ward in the hospital
At Bath.
Some nights she would come back to us
And sit and look straight out the window

Past the trees to other trees.
In the winter fog you would try to sleep
And the fog-horn at Small Point changed
The rhythm of your breathing. We lived in a 17th

Century parsonage and it did creak. The doorstone had
Lichen that shaded the stone into a face
Like an old man wearing a night-bonnet.
The Blaisdale's grandfather insisted it was

Reverend Cotter who died in the house in his sleep.
He was poisoned by a housekeeper.
She hanged herself
Out in the stable. And it was Cotter who planted

The lilac hedge outside my bedroom window,
When the wind came down from Sebasco Estates
My mother would jam the window with a dictionary
And all the rooms of the old house filled

With the smell of snapped lilac. Moose sometimes
Chewed at it. Once I woke in the morning
To the slobbering head of a cow moose through the window.
And my father during the week is at school in Bangor.

And my mother pale with her red hair rests,
At midnight, looking out the kitchen window where
All summer the fat moths were knocking their
Brains out against the lamp in the henhouse,

But now the moths are replaced with large
Flakes of snow, and there's no difference, moths
Or snow, for their lives are so short
That while they live they are already historical

Like a woman who knows too much about
The day before, who knows herself too well
There at the window, and who sadly
Touches a child's blue waterglass

As the old standing-clock in the hall begins
To slow and climb, slower and slower,
Through a thousand gears and ratchets
Into what she knew best, and

Into tomorrow.

THE PIANO

The first sentence is like pain if it remembers
The humid spangled pears of the summerhouse
At Shakhmatovo, or the dream you have in which

You dance with the Czar's youngest daughter:

She's dressed in a *mikado*-yellow shirt,
There's a long strand of hair in her mouth, and
As you dance, the steps you take together

Are suggested by the bullets that are just now

Tearing at her mouth and shoulder. And then it's
All repeated as she moves along a wall just behind
Her collapsed mother and father. She's shot, again,

And through the mouth and shoulder.

As you repeat these few movements your partner's
Eyes change to the white of egg-shells. The Czar
Was put in a plain cane-chair. There are still

The dusty country roads at Shakhmatovo.

Your first wife had heavy red hair, and as you
Dream the Duma sits like a crowd on the stairs:
At the center of the ballroom there are birches

Almost doubled over with wind. There's a white piano.

At night, St. Petersburg is empty, its lots vacant
Except for the purple iron fences standing
In blowing snow. You can only remember the folding

Canvas chair that looks out over

The choppy water just below Odessa. It's always
The same movements: she steps backwards, goes
Rigid, she shakes her head just once, and then

Slumps forward. There's blood on a *mikado*-yellow blouse.

There's blood in the horse-troughs of St. Petersburg.
And on the snow.
There's blood on the ivory keys of the piano.

She had heavy red hair and bluish elbows.

Blok, the streets of the city still run
With the iron trams, and baskets of lungwort
Are thrown for warmth over children who

Are sleeping in the open deserted buildings.

Once, when you were very young you watched peasants
Shoot a horse in a pasture: it fell over
Like a table. And what I've kept from you, Alexandr,

Is that you were cruel and handsome!

2.

You said that it only remains for us to fall asleep,
Or to break the window, how putting our heads out,
We could see life as being simple. Alright, then look

Down beneath you in the street: all other worlds

Repeat your simple life like down below you the deep,
Indigo, footprints in the snow. You sit and remember
Actresses with their long legs descending

An iron, spiral stairwell to their dressing-rooms

Where you flirted with them: empty bottles on a piano,
And roses bobbing in icewater. The mirrors are low.
You remember Lyubov': here in a dark room, each month

When she was bleeding her breath was scented as Petrograd is

This winter evening; her breasts grew big and sore.
You remember her, now, here in this dark room? Old; you sit
Like the servant who's unbuttoned his collar, who sits

Between two candles in the shadows, and picks

The last meat from the bones of a duck, or from
A dozen half-eaten milk-doves.
The large vase in the corner of the room is cracked.

I'm sorry, Alexandr, if you lack things.

I'm sorry for the poem is only important like a shoe!
Perhaps,
More like a pair of shoes. Or, say,

Like a blue, Etruscan slipper

Made of skins from the stomach of deer who were fed
Sweet-grasses and cress, and who were groomed
By virgins once each morning during an early spring.

A blue, Etruscan slipper like the frozen foot of the child

Sleeping below your window. His deep, indigo footprints.
This winter other lives repeat your complicated life.
His foot, you'd say, is elemental and real. You'd tell Lyubov'

It looked like a black, butchered seal;

With her child gone to the charnel-barn in Petersburg
She doesn't even hear you.
You are aware of her absence?

Her death came in the middle of a winter brook.

The child below your window has found
A large dry book. He'll burn it as fuel.
The blue smoke will reach your window. And, Alexandr,

You're forty: your teeth chatter as you run to look!

3.

The band falls silent. Behind you the beach
Goes gradually up to the road. You can see
In the seaweed some silver pepper-dulse tumble

Back as a big wave smooths out in front of you.

In Italy you dreamed you walked
Through fields of wheat and frankincense until
You came to a forest where women were waiting

With an old cow. *Alexandr, the band falls silent.*

There is the sound of water gurgling underground, and, once,

65

With Lyubov', at Shakhmatovo, you sat
In the dark parlor during a thunderstorm:

She bit into your shoulder and you slapped her face with

Some sheet music. You both laughed about it.
Walking outside afterwards she said
The air smelled clean like a German train.

She was pregnant, then, and wore a white scarf.

You both laughed, and there was blood at the side
Of her mouth and on your father's sheet music
Which was old and yellowed. *The band falls silent;*

And you are standing in an empty street in Rome

Screaming for a nasturtium with breasts. You were
Arrested that night,
And Lyubov' is dead, and Reghitza is a long way off!

The band became silent because you walked past them

With a tablecloth over your head, and just the one table
Falling over, you said, like a dead horse.
The horse was shot beside the ear, the ear fell off:

The horse spurting in the white saxifrage and tall grass.

The peasants walk off laughing. The head of the dead
Horse rested in a pool of blood. It looked like an anvil.
That night for supper there was

A thick, smoky roast on a platter surrounded by dark berries.

And, of course, you vomited.
The cook held your head
And then later she sang to you a lullaby in which

A young prince dies of a rose catarrh. It's not

A sad song. She nudged you a little and you frowned.
One night when you were just thirty
You stuck a revolver into your mouth. The night

Outside, you thought, was cold and ablative. A bird, then,

Flew into your room and the cat attacking it spilled
The vase in the corner.
Once, again, you laughed and grew older. It's always

The same like looking down a dark well in Spoleto:

You shouted your name and two boys ran out of the shadows.
The almond trees in wooden boxes are carried into
The streets, here, each Christmas. You chased the boys

Into an alley, still you are shouting your name.

It's like looking down into a well in Spoleto.
A band falls silent.
Or just a book flying through a window. The boy

Down below will burn it for fuel.

One night you beat Lyubov' to a pulp. Your shepherds
Have grey hair.
Gazing down into a dark well, at night, you felt

Something slip away. I think

You chased it into the alley. Calling out to it
You refused
To remember any of this by the morning

Which is Christmas Day. The almond trees *are* fragrant.

And, Alexandr, they said you hated the world in a new way.
After your mother and father divorced, he began
To write to you his dry, minatory letters,

Your mother once promised to hang herself with barbed wire.

And so something slid away while you shouted
Down into the dark well in Spoleto. It was
Like a sleigh with two horses pulling

Out of the gate to your grandfather's house

Outside Moscow. Try to understand! You lived
On the edge of a city: its people, now, file
Past your grave: they raise their collars, they drop flowers,

And they say your poems aloud with tenderness: the way, drunk,
You would say the list of names of women you had shamed.

JACOB BOEHME'S TRIPTYCH OF
WINTER HOURS: 1620

For my brother

There is fog in a meadow where bluebirds
Are wheeling and turning in the cold space:
There are young plane trees in snow looking
Like bell ropes that come out of low ceilings
From nowhere:
A thing can be desired only if it has
An opposite to resist it.
There could not be light without darkness.
There could not be good without evil.
There could not be a water crust in the well
Or a white light high up in the oak groves.
One warm summer night I
Left a pail of milk
Out on a windowsill to cool, and

I sat down at my table with friends
And put a lighted candle
On the blue, plated back of a wood louse
And announced that this plough-horse of an insect
Would soon cross over all the way to the opposite
Edge of the table, but, you would say, what if the louse
Having reached the other edge had flown off
And out of the open window with Boehme's candle!
Would there have been, then, two morning stars
For your children?
Late that night with just the light of
This candlestick I finished
The sentence I had begun nearly a year ago.
I wrote: and the ale is warm, as

The wings of this almost colorless insect are beating
With double vision, everywhere at once, the wings
Have become a waterwheel barely
Turning in a frozen stream beside a mill;
The illusion of the wings, now, is solid
Like a millstone *itself:*
A starling screams out in the purple brambles,
And can the beginning go to the end without
Beginning again, not like my wood louse dragged
Back again and again for my friends:
How he beat his wings, but then
The hot wax flooding down on him
Caught him in its cold form and just
Once more he painfully lifted his wings, and let

Them fall as an angel, petals of an oxeye daisy,
Or as two walls of a barn breaking in with heavy snow!